A GOLDEN SOUVENIR OF
TEMPLES OF THAILAND

A
GOLDEN
SOUVENIR
OF THE

TEMPLES

OF THAILAND

THEIR FORM AND FUNCTION

Photography and Text by Michael Freeman

ASIA BOOKS

Published and distributed in Thailand by Asia Books Co. Ltd.,
5 Soi 61 Sukhumvit Rd., Bangkok, Thailand
P.O. Box 40, Bangkok 10110
Tel. 392-0910, 391-0590
Fax. (662) 381-1621, 391-2277

Produced by Pacific Rim Press (H.K.) Ltd.
©1991, Pacific Rim Press (H.K.) Ltd., Hong Kong. All rights reserved.
Tel. (852) 2856-3896
Fax. (852) 2565-8004

Reprinted 1994, 1996

(Title page)
The gilded Phra Sri Ratana Chedi in Bangkok's royal temple complex, Wat Phra Kaeo.

(Right)
A gilded screen detail at Wat Po, the country's largest temple.

(Pages 6-7)
Night-time offerings at the base of the famous northern chedi *at Wat Prathat Lampang Luang, during the Yi Peng festival. In the north of the country, this is the equivalent of Loy Krathong, the Thai festival of the November full moon.*

(Pages 8-9)
Illuminated for the 1987 celebrations in honour of King Bhumibol's 60th birthday, the chedis *and spires of Wat Phra Kaeo, with the Grand Palace behind, glow and sparkle under a full moon. Built at the end of the eighteenth century by Rama I, Wat Phra Kaeo is within the grounds of the royal palace, overlooking the Sanam Luang.*

(Pages 10-11)
Like an island in a sea of green ricefields, Wat Po Thong Charoen in the Mae Ping Valley has the typical appearance of a country temple, set apart from the surrounding hamlets.

Text and photography by Michael Freeman

Edited by Nick Wallwork

Typeset by Bothwin Typesetting Centre
Artwork by Aubrey Tse, Au Yeung Chui Kwai

Printed in China by Twin Age Ltd.

ISBN 962-217-399-3

INTRODUCTION

When Siddhartha Gautama died in northern India in 543BC, he left behind a doctrine that had a profound effect on most of Asian Buddhism. A remarkable philosopher in a country that had no shortage of holy men, he achieved such a perfect understanding of existence that he became known as the Buddha—the Enlightened. Although the religion that grew from his teachings later disappeared in India, it spread out to take hold in other countries, changing society, beliefs and, inevitably, art and architecture.

Thailand's legacy is Theravada Buddhism, the more traditional of the two forms of the religion. It dispenses with the idea of a God—only human effort can improve existence and reach salvation. The Buddha showed the way and is the supreme teacher and guide. One of its major tenets is that good and evil in one life bear fruit in the next, making it essential to build up a store of merit by appropriate actions. The focus of this belief, and of Buddhist teaching, is the temple, and in Thailand there are twenty-seven thousand of these, nearly all thoroughly active. Together, they embody much of the traditional Thai way of life, providing a unique, unforgettable part of the landscape.

Although 'temple' is the closest word in English, it does not really convey the full meaning of the word as used in Thailand. It conjures up the idea of simply a place of worship, a sort of exotic church, whereas a Thai temple is much more. Unlike most other religions, which have a large laity and small ministry, Buddhism requires all male adherents to enter the monkhood—the *Sangha*, as it is called—for at least a short period of their lives. As a result, a Thai temple is as much a monastery as place of prayer. In a country where religion has a deep influence on daily life, culture and education, the temple is very much a community centre. The Thai name—*wat*—refers to all of the buildings within the temple compound.

Buddhism arrived in Thailand in the third century BC from two different routes: from the north and from the south. The two sects, increasingly divergent in the way they interpreted the teachings of Gautama, were Theravada and Mahayana. Theravada was, and remains, the more traditional; in Mahayana Buddhism there developed a pantheon of other figures to worship, notably the *bodhisattvas* (literally 'Buddhas-to-

A distinctive feature of most Thai wats is the chedi which is often referred to as a stupa *or* pagoda *in English. Ultimately derived from the Indian* tumulus, chedis *are the housings for sacred relics of the Buddha. Here, the chedi of Wat Saen Fang in the heart of Chiangmai shows the strong Burmese influence typical of many nineteenth century temples built in the area.*

The gilded hands of a divinity grace the doors of a chapel at Wat Chieng Man (opposite).

13

Decorative temple details are as varied as the number of wats, frequently showing an eclectic choice of materials and techniques. This small selection includes mother-of-pearl inlay in a door at Bangkok's Wat Rajabopit, a modern mosaic of mirror and glass at Wat Chieng Man in Chiangmai, and European-influenced tiles, also at Wat Rajabopit.

be'). Bodhisattvas are beings who, having followed the Buddha's precepts, reach the point of total enlightenment yet hold back from taking the final step so that they can remain on Earth to help mankind. In Thailand, Theravada Buddhism first gained a foothold in the area around present-day Nakhon Pathom, and was accepted by the Mons, who settled in the Lower Menam Valley before the arrival of the Thais. In the south and the east, the Mahayana sect dominated, but by the thirteenth century, it was the state religion of the Khmer Empire, which by then ruled a large part of what is now Thailand. The matter was effectively settled in the middle of the thirteenth century with the establishment of the first independent Thai kingdom—Khmer rule was overthrown, and Sukhothai became the first capital. King Li Thai, grandson of Ramkhamhaeng, assembled the Theravada Buddhist scriptures into one volume, the *Tribhumikatha*.

Theravada Buddhism, although followed by more than nine-tenths of the Thai population, does not have an exclusive hold on the religious attentions of the community. Over the centuries during which it was introduced, there already existed Brahmanism (principally for the ruling classes) and the older animism of ordinary people. The result is a mixture that persists today. Brahmanic rituals, for example, continue in forms little altered from the practices of the Khmers, particularly in royal ceremonies. One such is the Ploughing Ceremony, which takes place in front of the Grand Palace on the Sanam Luang, and is intended to bless the beginning of rice planting. Presided over by the King, the ceremony involves a ritual ploughing by oxen, which at the end select from a choice of seven foods, and in doing so predict the harvest to come. All this is administered by Brahman priests, to the sound of conch shells, an enduring Hindu symbol.

Although Buddhism is nominally the practised religion, the mythology of Brahmanism and the numerous spirits from animism are woven in, and play an important part in the temples and their decorations. Images of the Buddha naturally have pride of place, but the serpents, monsters, female dancers and gods that adorn murals, bas-reliefs and so on are the representatives of older worship. The Thais have been quite happy to hold on to what they see as the best parts of other faiths, and following the teachings of the Buddha has not prevented most people from praying to minor deities when the occasion demands.

In a larger sense, the uniqueness of Thai temple architecture springs from the country's position in Asia. With Burma, India and Sri Lanka to the west, Cambodia in the east, China and Laos to the north, Thailand has been peculiarly susceptible to the cross-currents of culture and religion. Most of its neighbours are devoutly Buddhist (or at least have been until very recently), and their regional traits have flowed through Thailand with the shifts of power and movements of peoples across Southeast Asia. The Sri Lankan stupa can be seen in the Thai bell-shaped *chedi*, Khmer sanctuary towers are the centre-pieces of the main sites in northeastern Thailand, while the richly carved, broad teak halls of Laos are mirrored in the style of northern Thailand. The Thai temple has managed to accommodate all of these, and more.

For the first-time visitor all this variety, although spectacular, can be more than a little confusing. It adds enormously to the pleasure of looking at temples simply to be able to identify the types of building and to know something of the way they are used. Let's find a typical wat to walk around.

This alone poses something of a problem, as no two are exactly the same—the one described here is something of an amalgamation. One reason for the variety of design and layout is apparent the moment we enter the gate from the street: there is not one building, but a whole compound full of them. Unlike, say, a Burmese temple in which practically everything is housed under one roof (or a Christian church, for that matter), a Thai wat is more of a temple complex. This in turn has led to the practice of new buildings being added at different times—there is no architectural need to plan the layout all at once. Ad hoc growth is a characteristic feature, although it can be a little disorienting at first, it also means that Thai temples are full of surprises.

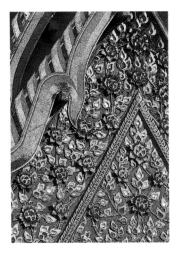

We should try and enter through the east gate. Traditionally, this is the principal entrance, facing the sunrise, although there are others in the wall that encloses the compound. In front of us are likely to be two buildings similar in shape, although not necessarily in size. One is the ordination hall—known in Thai as the *bot*, or *ubosot*. The other is the assembly, or prayer hall, and called the *viharn* by Thais. Distinguishing one from the other takes a little prior knowledge: the bot is surrounded by eight boundary stones, set at each corner and at the four cardinal points. These stones, typically flat like leaves and known as *bai sema*, mark the limits of consecrated ground. The bot is not a public building, and more than this, under normal circumstances, women are forbidden to enter (in the more visited wats there are notice signs to this effect).

Most, but not all, temples have a bot, and it is the most important building in the temple. It should face east, and if possible water (the Buddha achieved enlightenment facing a river). Typically, it is rectangular, with a tall narrow main doorway in one end and an uneven number of small windows along each side. It is the roof, however, that immediately catches the eye; overlapping and multi-tiered, it has come to symbolise Thai architecture in the Western imagination.

The upper section of the roof is steeply angled, but this overlaps lower sections that have a successively shallower pitch, so that the overall effect is of an upward sweeping curve, like a flaring skirt. Indeed, the rafters on some bots are themselves curved. Not only does the roof overlap in sections at the sides, but at each end it is also tiered. The whole combination of stacked sections of roof creates an impression of both delicacy in what is basically a substantial building, and of upward movement.

However, while it is easy to read an aesthetic purpose into these remarkable buildings, in reality they have evolved over a very long period and no-one really knows how the features were developed. The overlapping of roofs so that the lower sections project well beyond the walls at a shallower angle was probably originally devised as a way of protecting the foundations from heavy run-off during the monsoons. But the distinctive tiering: does it have religious significance or is it for more practical reasons? Archaeological evidence offers some clues. The two earliest civilisations in Southeast Asia about which there is an architectural record, date from around the second and third centuries BC: the Bronze Age *Dong Son* culture centred on North Vietnam and the *Dian* culture in Yunnan. Bronze artifacts such as containers and drums, have been found decorated with pictures of houses. These show tiered roofs, gable ends that project slightly beyond the ends of the building and a roofline that dips in the centre—almost certainly because of sagging beams.

The gable ends of buildings, and in particular those of viharns, *have traditionally been areas for intricate decoration and religious symbolism. Many of these symbols pre-date Buddhist beliefs; the white-toothed grimacing face is that of a* kala, *a demon which, according to Hindu legend, was commanded to devour itself. It appears as a guardian over entrances.*

Characteristic feature of Thai temple architecture. The most common mythological creature is the naga, *At Wat Nantaram in Chiangmai (top), nagas cascade down the viharn's multi-tiered roof; a single naga (bottom) adorns the end of a viharn at Wat Si Khom Kham in Phayao. The florally-derived finial in the centre is called a* ngao.

The bas-reliefs of one of Southeast Asia's most important monuments, the Bayon in the temple complex of Angkor, carry detailed views of thirteenth century buildings. These roofs are virtually identical to those of modern Thai, Cambodian and Laotian temples and palaces. They are multi-tiered, the profiles of the gable ends curve down gracefully and end with upswept projections, and there are exactly the same decorations. Built in wood, these buildings have long since disappeared, but the stone record survives.

One of the most remarkable things about the architectural history of the temples, is how little they have changed over the centuries. There is a strongly conservative streak, itself not so unusual in religious design. As the noted French architect Jacques Dumarcay says, 'There is little real structural difference . . . between the tiered roofs of a Bronze Age dwelling in Yunnan and those found in contemporary Thai architecture.'

Although these ancient buildings lacked decoration, roof ornaments were being applied liberally by the time of the Khmer civilisation of Angkor. There were finials everywhere: along the ridges, at the ridge-ends and at the gable ends. This characteristic punctuation of the roof line remains to this day. In fact, these finials are our first introduction to the symbolism that runs through all temple architecture in Thailand—not all of it to do with Buddhism. There are two kinds of finial. Standing at one end of the bot, we can see at the corner of each roof-eave the rearing head of a serpent. This is the *naga*, a mythological creature that appears time and again in all kinds of decorative motifs, with origins in Hindu religion. The naga is, in fact, a water-serpent, and the serrated ridge that runs from the peak of the roof down to the head is its body. It puts in other appearances elsewhere, as eave brackets, for example, and occasionally as an undulating balustrade to steps.

The finial at the peak of the roof ridge is the *chofa*, a more enigmatic symbol. There is no complete agreement about its origins or meaning, and even its name can be interpreted differently—as 'bouquet in the sky' or 'celestial realm'. In some temples it appears as a mythical swan, in others as an abstract horn, in yet others as a naga. One thing is certain, however: it is the one essential adornment for a bot or viharn.

Architecturally, the viharn is much the same as the bot, even though it may be larger or smaller, and show any number of individual characteristics. Inside, too, the two buildings follow similar lines. At the end farthest from the main entrance is the image, or several images, of the Buddha. To support the complex arrangement of beams and rafters (often exposed to view in northern temples) there may be two rows of columns running the length of the interior, leaving a kind of broad aisle down the middle. Ceiling and walls may be left as plain white stucco, or else decorated and painted. The viharn is where the laity worship and gather to hear monks reading the scriptures.

Somewhere within the compound—often behind the viharn—there is likely to be a *chedi*, another characteristic and beautiful Thai structure. Known formerly as a stupa, its origins lie far back in India as a burial mound, and it is essentially a housing for relics. The most sacred chedis are those containing relics of the Buddha himself. If the temple has a chedi this important, it will be reflected in its name, which will include the words *Phra That* (Buddha Relic) or *Mahathat* (Great Relic). Chedis vary a great deal in style and detail, but one of the most typical forms is the bell shape, originally from Sri Lanka. Above the platform and base, often square, is the hemispherical part called the *anda*—literally 'egg' in Sanskrit, as some early stupas had an oval section. Above this is a pedestal known as the *harmika*, which in turn supports a tapering stack of rings—the slender pinnacle called the *chattravali*. Two of Bangkok's best known chedis—the gilded Phra Si Ratana in Wat Phra Kaeo and the Golden Mount—have this structure. Over the centuries, temple architects have developed and adapted this basic theme. One distinctive kind of stupa is topped with a bulb-like lotus bud (the central monument at Sukhothai has this form). Another design, very different from the chedi, is the *prang*, which looks rather like a giant corn cob and is descended from the Khmer sanctuary towers found in archaeological sites in the north-east of the country.

There are likely to be other buildings around the compound. As a monastery there are, of course, living quarters for the monks, but nowadays these tend to be architecturally undistinguished. There may be a building for public use, with a decorated roof in the style of the bot and viharn, but without walls. This is the *sala*, a combination of meeting hall and shelter. Travellers can sleep here overnight.

In the temple we are visiting there is also an intriguing structure close to the bot. Reminiscent of a miniature bot, it is raised high on a tall, narrow base, and reached by a small, steep stairway. This is the *haw-trai*, or library for sacred texts. Its elevation is a protection against flooding and other dangers, although now its importance is mainly symbolic, as the scriptures tend to be kept elsewhere. Other buildings that we might find are a schoolhouse (some temples still provide education for local children), a bell-tower, and a *mondop*, which is a square building housing a Buddha image or relic (and which would take the place of a chedi).

The styles of temple buildings have been influenced over the centuries by all of Thailand's neighbours. In some periods this has produced very distinctive architecture, preserved in the country's great historical monuments such as Sukhothai, Ayutthaya and the Khmer sites like Phimai and Phanom Rung. On a more modest scale, certain motifs and lines can be seen lingering in the details of a temple. In one viharn, for example, the windows might have turned vertical bars; this design comes from the Khmer. In another temple, elephants surround the base of the chedi; this is a Singhalese influence, reminiscent of the great stupa at Anuradhapura in Sri Lanka.

The ultimate source of most of this was India, but filtered through other cultures: Sri Lanka, Mon from southern Burma, Srivijaya from Sumatra, Khmer from what is now Cambodia, and Pagan from central Burma. More recently, Chinese and even European influences can be seen in Bangkok temples. Each of these styles made itself felt at a different period of history, and in different parts of the country, while Thailand itself has had more than one renaissance of art and architecture. From the end of the 13th century to the beginning of the 15th, the kingdom of Sukhothai flourished in the central plains, and with it a style that integrated all of the previous foreign influences. Then, from the middle of the 14th century to the 18th the kingdom and art of Ayutthaya blossomed, absorbing Sukhothai. In the last two centuries, since the founding of Bangkok, temple styles have been named after the modern royal dynasty—*Rattanakosin*.

More beings from Hindu mythology, of varying idiosyncracy, decorate a variety of temples: from top to bottom, at Wat Donsak, Lap Lae; Wat Trimit in Bangkok; and Wat San Pakoi in Chiangmai.

17

Costly and time-consuming temple restoration was given a boost by the 1982 Bangkok Bicentennial celebrations, and the momentum has continued ever since. The focus of the celebrations was Rattanakosin Island in Bangkok, at its centre the Grand Palace and Wat Phra Kaeo. Here, workers from the Fine Arts Department restore the giant figure of a garuda (called krut *in Thai), the half-man half-bird mount of the god Vishnu; others re-gild the multi-ringed spire of the Phra Sri Ratana Chedi.*

One of the reasons why Thai temples are so exuberant in shape, colour and detail is that most influences have been added, and very little subtracted. Motif and decorative technique are often piled on top of each other. Even so, while it is possible to detect some of these strains running through the country's temples, for the most part they remain no more tangible than that. Relatively few buildings are of great age. This is partly because of the materials used—for the most part wood, brick and stucco until the modern period of concrete. None of these is very durable and wooden beams and posts in particular need regular replacement.

But there is a more important reason. Drive along any country road or walk through a town and you are likely to see construction work going on in at least one temple. In its new prosperity, the entire country is addicted to construction, but in the temples it has always been so. There are many ways of making merit in a Buddhist society, but one of the most guaranteed is to put up a new temple structure. Western ideas about conservation at all levels of building do not apply to anything like the same extent. In Europe at least, churches and cathedrals tend to be seen as things to preserve. In Thailand, the attitude is rather more functional. Buildings like the viharn serve a purpose, and indeed are in daily use. If a sturdy construction of concrete serves the purpose better than decaying timber and flaking stucco, why not rebuild entirely? And as the new work carries considerable merit, so much the better.

It seems sad to many Westerners that old structures are pulled down rather than restored (and, to be fair, to an increasing number of Thais), but the temple complex is a dynamic entity. This constant tinkering with temple architecture is nothing new and neither is the reaction. An English guidebook of 1924 complained that 'the country is dotted with wats in every stage of dilapidation and decay, and also with many cheap constructions whose ugliness makes them so many blots upon the landscape.' The concrete revolution has since then completely altered the construction methods, and the speed with which new temples can be built has heightened the problem—architectural style is undoubtedly suffering. It is no longer necessary to rely on craftsmen and builders skilled in temple construction, and less time and care is lavished on design and ornamentation.

Improvement and restoration are fine in principle, but what is steadily being lost in this process is important temple architecture from the past. What has yet to catch up with Thailand's new economic boom is an effective sense of conservation. Many of the best architectural features of country wats—gable ends, pillars, chofas, eave brackets and so on—sadly find their way to Bangkok and Chiangmai antique dealers. The pieces themselves will undoubtedly be well preserved, but out of context and scattered around the world.

Nevertheless, despite these losses, there still remains a wealth of fine temple architecture, as the sampling in this book shows. The more that these are seen to be appreciated and enjoyed by visitors, the better chance they have of being preserved. The big-city wats are in little danger, but the smaller countryside temples are much less in the public eye and deserve more attention.

In fact, for all the spectacle and splendour of the great wats of Bangkok—the first that most visitors see—it is the small village wats that most closely evoke the experience of Thai temple life. The country is still predominantly rural, and it is there that the special relationship between the temple and the lay community continues. When Buddhism first came to Thailand, the monks were travellers, walking from village to village. With the onset of the rainy season, which made travel difficult, they stopped with one community, which housed and supported them. From these plain beginnings the monasteries grew. Through meditation and prayer, the monks increase the spiritual well-being of the whole community, and the wat itself provides all kinds of ways for the villagers to increase their merit—by doing work for the temple, making offerings and worship. Besides this, the monks are not totally separate from the community. Every Buddhist male should at some time in his life be ordained as a monk, if only for a few months or weeks. Nowadays not everyone does, but the tradition is most closely followed in the countryside. At any one time, a temple will contain a mixture of resident monks—some who have made it their lifetime calling, together with those whose stay is just for the rainy season.

In a sense, the ordination of men and boys from the surrounding settlements epitomises the links between the wat and the community. There is a direct involvement, in both directions. The wat is a part of the life and experience of the people, who support it practically and in prayer. In return, the wat cares for their spiritual well-being. For those Western visitors who take the time to experience something of Thai life it is the strong communal bonds between religion and society that is the most impressive feature of wats. The architecture and its decoration are naturally eye-catching and have an instant appeal, but both are actually a reflection of a religion that plays an unusually strong, but benign, role in daily life.

A carved teak bracket in the form of a naga serpent (above), *supports the overhanging roof eaves of the viharn at Wat San Pakoi in Chiangmai* (below).

Temple settings range from grand to modest, from the heart of cities to isolated countryside. One of the most impressive sites of all temples is that of Wat Prathat Lampang Luang in the North. Built as a fortified temple, or **wiang**, it rises over the surrounding countryside, protected by moats and ramparts. It was once the site of a famous engagement in the eighteenth century against occupying Burmese forces, and now holds important ceremonies, particularly at the November Yi Peng, shown here under a full moon (left).

The Burmese-style Wat Chong Klang (top) sits between ricefields and a small lake at the edge of the small town of Mae Hong Son in one of the most picturesque of settings. Less architecturally significant, a gaudily painted **wat** (right) on the outskirts of Chiangmai serves the needs of a small local community. In the heart of Bangkok, Wat Po (above) is both the largest in the country and the oldest in the capital.

(Previous page)
In the middle of ricefields and palms at the foot of the 2,230m (7,540ft) mountain of Doi Chiang Dao, the viharn of a rural temple glows in the late afternoon sun.

The essential building in a temple complex is the bot *(or more formally, the* ubosot*), used among other things for the ordination of monks. Built on sacred ground demarcated by boundary stones, it is commonly closed to visitors, and always to women. The bot above, built in typical sturdy Lanna style, is in the village of Ban Chae Son, north of Lampang. The boundary stone, (left) known in Thai as a* bai sema, *is, by contrast, at the late-nineteenth century temple of Wat Borworniwet in Bangkok.*

Wat Chiang Man (right) is one of the oldest still-functioning temples, having been built by King Mengrai in 1297. The fine bot is, like all wooden temple buildings, much more recent; nevertheless, dating from the nineteenth century it is relatively old for a teak building. The legacy of multi-tiered roofs like this stretches in an unbroken line back to at least the second century BC in southern China.

(Left)

In its basic architecture, the viharn is often indistinguishable from the bot; each have the characteristic multi-tiered, skirted and flaring roof. The viharn, being essentially an assembly hall, is more often than not larger than the bot, which is put to more limited ritual uses, but there are many exceptions to this. Viharns, however, are never surrounded by the bai sema that mark the consecrated ground. This flamboyantly designed viharn at Wat San Pakoi in Chiangmai is approached by a double curving stairway, guarded by a naga balustrade.

Not only does the end of the viharn offer the architect an area for ornamentation, but this setting for the entrance marks a transition between the secular and the religious. Thai temple artists have always taken this opportunity to elaborate the entrance, as for example in the square panels of a gable end (top) and the 'eyebrow' spandrel over a portico (right).

The functions of a viharn include the housing of specially revered images of the Buddha. This group of images (top) is housed between wooden pillars at the end of the Viharn Nam Tam at Wat Prathat Lampang Luang; built in the sixteenth century, this open-sided viharn is widely considered to be the country's oldest wooden building. The viharn is used by the local community for worship (left); shoes are always removed before entering any temple building (above).

At the renowned Wat Phrathat Si Chomthong (right), candles in traditional clay containers are ranged outside the sixteenth-century viharn, rebuilt in 1817. They mark the start of the November Loy Krathong celebrations.

Libraries, known as haw trai in Thai, evolved as special buildings to house manuscripts and keep them secure. Before printed texts were widely available, each wat needed its own copy of Buddhist doctrines as well as magical diagrams and instructions for preparing medicines. These texts were traditionally written on palm-leaf manuscripts, which were then bound and stored in wooden chests. The basic architectural form is similar to that of the viharn and bot, but on a smaller scale; an elevated base, as in this library at Wat Haripoonchai (left) in Lamphun offers some protection against insects.

Palm-leaf manuscripts are still used for readings of Buddhist scriptures in the viharn (above), although the manuscripts themselves are no longer stored in the haw trai. Another, even smaller building in some wats is the bell-tower; (right), a lay helper strikes the bell for noon.

The distinctive skirting and tiering of the roofs of temple buildings has a long history within Southeast Asia, and may have derived from a need to protect the foundations from heavy monsoonal rains. For many centuries, however, the roof design has been institutionalised. The orange, ochre, green, red and white are typical of Bangkok wats. The roof edges are decorated with nagas, often gilded; their bodies run down from the ridge and their heads rear up above the eaves. The other essential roof decoration at the ridge end is a finial known as a chofa (right), which can be abstract in form, or in the shape of a swan, naga, or even an elephant. Some temples have finials in the form of semi-divinities (above).

Great attention to detail, often highly elaborate, is lavished on doorways. Typical of the more baroque styles is the door to the viharn of *Wat Puak Hong* (opposite) in Chiangmai. The ornate gilded stucco of the portal shows one of the basic differences between northern and central Thai designs: in the north, emphasis is usually given to the pediment above the door, while in central Thailand the door panels themselves normally receive most of the ornament. In another northern viharn (top), rectangular carved panels on the gable-end surmount a door pediment with a looping 'eyebrow' shape, forming a shallow portico.

Another characteristic door decoration is the makara arch, derived from the Khmer architecture of Angkor. The two curves of this arch are represented by the bodies of makaras (mythical sea-monsters) which at the base of the arch spew out nagas from their mouths. This distinctive arch shape is repeated even in modern frames such as *Wat Chieng Man* (left).

Gold has always played an important part in temple art and architecture. Gilding is the most common means of applying gold, and, in the form of finely beaten, tissue-thin gold leaf squares, is an affordable way for worshippers to pay homage to revered images, as at Wat Phra Kaeo (top). Significant chedis (considered to house genuine relics of the Buddha) are often gilded, as at the fifteenth century chedi at Wat Haripoonchai in Lamphun (left).

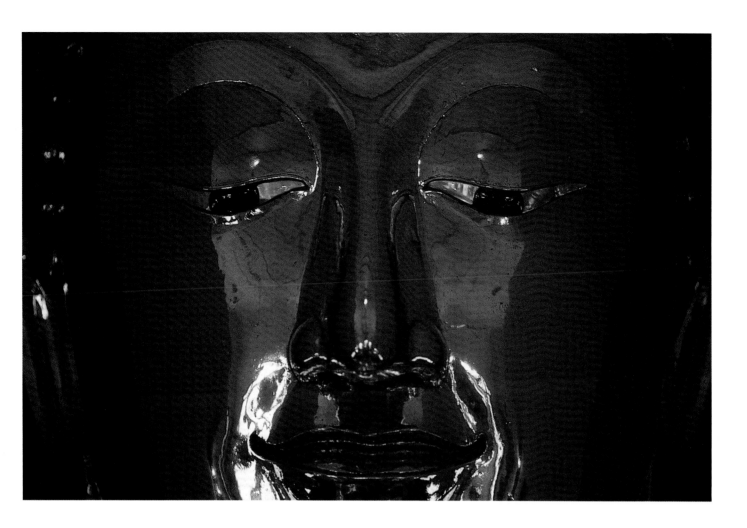

The most famous of all golden images in Thailand is the so-called Golden Buddha (top) in Wat Trimit, located in Bangkok's Chinatown. Three metres (nine feet) high and weighing five and a half tons, it was covered in stucco to disguise and protect it from the invading Burmese army in the eighteenth century. Its true nature was discovered only by accident, when it slipped while being moved by crane and the stucco cracked, revealing the gold underneath.

At Wat Bowornivet, famous for being the temple at which kings and royal princes spend their monastic retreat, gilding enhances the fine Sukhothai statue of Phra Buddha Chinasara (the smaller of the two at right).

Chedis, or reliquary towers, were built to house sacred relics or the remains of kings, princes or famous members of the sangha (the Buddhist monkhood). The forms vary, but most are essentially conical, solid structures tapering to a spire. The rounded bell shape, seen in silhouette against an evening sky (opposite) at Chiangmai's Wat Suan Dok, is the most typical. Another style, common in the north, is Burmese, with a relatively broad base (top). Surmounting the chedi's spire (left) is an honorific umbrella, called chat in Thai, which evolved from the royal multi-tiered parasol.

While the majority of the country's chedis are relatively unadorned with surface detail, some are highly elaborate. Making merit through the building of new chedis (or the alteration of existing ones), Burmese residents introduced an ornate rococo style, as can be seen in a detail of the painted stucco-work of Wat Saen Fang (left). Gold is used for important chedis, such as that at Doi Suthep (top).

A different evolution marks the other distinctive tower shape in Thai religious architecture—the prang. Shaped like a corn cob, as in the fine example at Wat Mahathat in Phitsanuloke (bottom), the rounded tower derives from the Khmer sanctuary towers and the twelfth century style of Angkor Wat.

41

Wats are monasteries as much as places of worship, and the saffron robes of monks are a constant reminder of the scale of Buddhism in Thai life. Opposite, two newly ordained monks carry on their backs their newly acquired alms bowls, which they will use for collecting offerings of rice from the community.

The ordination itself (above) takes place at the beginning of the Buddhist Lent, and all Thai males are supposed to undertake this. Young novices (below) receiving an education at Wat Po in Bangkok, take a break from their studies in the middle of the day.

The sangha, or monkhood (above), is also portrayed in temple
art, as in the statue opposite and as depicted on a carved door
panel (below).

A Thai male is not considered to be a complete man until he has been ordained and has spent at least a nominal period in a wat; until then he is, in Thai idiom, an 'unripe person'. Ordination ceremonies traditionally take place at kao pansa, the start of Lent and the beginning of the rainy season; those for whom this is a rite of passage rather than a lifetime's calling will spend a few weeks or months at the wat.

In the early morning of the day of ordination, the young man's head and eyebrows are shaved. He is then carried on the shoulders of friends to the wat, dressed in white (symbolic of purity). The procession then walks around the bot three times; inside, the participants promise to adhere to the ten precepts of novice monks, and are dressed in saffron robes.

Daily life in a wat for the resident monks is a mixture of domestic housekeeping, meditation and instruction. In the early morning sunlight, a young monk hangs washed robes on a line to dry (top); in Lamphun (above and left), school occupies most of the novices' day.

Early each morning, starting before dawn, a common sight throughout Thailand is that of monks, individually and in groups, collecting rice from the laity. This is in no way begging; on the contrary, it is considered a privilege and an opportunity for the layman to make merit. Novices at the wat prepare the food for senior monks (above and right); the day's eating must be completed before noon.

Some wats have unusual and idiosyncratic roles: an hour or two upriver from the capital, Wat Phai Lom, on the banks of the Chaophaya River, has become a sanctuary for Openbill storks, migrating annually from the north. Elsewhere, they are in danger of being shot by farmers, but here they are welcomed; birds injured from falls are tended, here (top left) by the Abbot of Wat Phai Lom. Taking full advantage of the sanctuary, an adult stork (below) raids the roof of a temple building for nesting material.

A few wats have developed as religious theme parks in a uniquely Thai manner. The largest is Wat Phai Rong Wua, northwest of Bangkok. Concrete statuary over a large area is intended to demonstrate basic moral behaviour, its rewards and punishments. A park of several hundred concrete Buddha images (top) stuns the visitor with its scale; more vivid imagination, however, has been applied to the punishments awaiting sinners: (right) a giant blue demon casts newcomers to Hell into a boiling cauldron.

Temples are also a focus for worship and the making of merit. At Wat Po, the giant reclining Buddha attracts a constant stream of people offering prayers (opposite). At Wat Haripoonchai, the end of the rainy season is marked, as in temples all over the country, with the Thot Kathin festival (above and below). This is the principal occasion for the public to make merit by making offerings.

While Thai temples are Buddhist, the religious beliefs include important undercurrents from Hinduism and even earlier forms of animism, fortune-telling and superstition. Largely free from uncompromising dogma, Thai Buddhism accepts these other forms of worship, and the result is a fascinating syncretic blend. Spirit houses (above and left), a feature of all Thai dwellings, are also found in the grounds of many wats. They are built to house the displaced spirit of the place.

In the grounds of Wat Mahathat in Phitsanuloke, a fortune-teller spreads her cards out for temple visitors (opposite). Fortune-telling is taken very seriously by most Thais.

The attitude of prayer is a common sight within the temple precincts, and a recurrent theme in temple art— in murals and gilded door panels, for example.

The lotus features in many legends concerning the Buddha, and indeed plays an important part in Hindu cosmology; it is frequently held in prayer (above).

Lay members of the community can make merit by performing services for the temple. At Mae Cham in the north, people from as far away as Bangkok have contributed to the restoration of the temple buildings (top), and attend the inauguration at Thot Kathin. The end of harvest in Chiangmai frees local farmers from their land for a short time; some donate their services as sculptors in concrete to make new Buddha images for a nearby wat (left).

Just as the laity provide practical services for the wat, so the monks conduct various ceremonies for the community. In a private house, monks from the wat perform a ceremony to bless the dwelling, its inhabitants and ancestors (top); in Lap Lae, near Uttaradit (below), a ceremony attended by most of the village is intended to dispel the causes of misfortune that had recently struck the community. The string carries the power of the monks' prayers.

The mythology of the naga (or nak as it is called in Thai) appeared in India more than two thousand years ago but may have even more ancient and primitive origins. In Sanskrit, naga means serpent, and in the Hindu epics of the Mahabharata and the Puranas, the nagas were a powerful race, half-human and half-snake. The appearance of the naga Mucalinda, who sheltered the Buddha during the latter's meditation, confirmed its place in Thai religious symbolism. In wats it is seen chiefly in roof decoration and as undulating balustrades.

A range of mythological references greatly enriches the decorative interest of Thai wats. At Wat Po, a sequence of 152 marble bas-relief panels (top) illustrate the well-loved legend of the Ramakien. This is the Thai version of the Ramayana, a kind of Hindu Iliad, originally written more than two thousand years ago by the poet Valmiki.

The half-human kinnari, with the head and torso of a woman and the wings and legs of a bird, appears in a stucco panel along the walls of Wat Saen Fang's viharn (below). In mythology, they inhabited the forested lower slopes of the Himalayas.

Portal guardians (opposite) protect some temples from the entry of devils. Those with the fierce, intimidating faces of monsters are yaksas. Here, one such statue guards the viharn of Wat Phrathat Si Chomthong.

Wats are the focal point of many popular festivals. On this page, Loy Krathong is celebrated in different ways at different temples. At Wat Benjamabopit (opposite), the birth, enlightenment and death of the Buddha is celebrated at Visakha Puja.

In the hottest part of the year, villages in Thailand's Northeast perform an intriguing rain-making propitiation—the Rocket Festival, in which black-powder rockets are launched. The biggest celebration is at Yasothon, where not only does the grand parade end at one of the town's wats (opposite), but many of the rockets are actually built in temple precincts (above).

At the famous northern temple of Wat Haripoonchai in Lamphun, the year's major festival is Ngan Salagabat, featuring a number of curious rites. The public bring offerings of all kinds, including ten-baht notes in cleft sticks and packets of washing powder; some are loaded onto an 'offerings tree' (opposite). Other features include elaborate model houses commemorating the deceased (right).

The two most important temples in the country flank the Grand Palace in the heart of Bangkok: Wat Phra Kaeo and Wat Po. The former (left) was built at the start of the present Royal dynastic period by King Rama I and epitomises the baroque and regal splendour of the Rattanakosin style. Elaborate ornamentation extends even to the tiniest detail, as in the exquisite mother-of-pearl inlay in a chapel's doors (top).

A wealth of colour decorates these Rattanakosin temples: gilded roof ornaments (top left), gaudily painted Yaksa guardian giants (top right), the pearly irridescence of an elephant set into the feet of the Reclining Buddha (bottom left), and the frescoes lining the cloisters of Wat Phra Kaeo (bottom right).

The inspiration for the building of Wat Phra Kaeo was the need to house the country's most sacred religious icon—the Emerald Buddha (opposite). In reality made of green jasper, the 75cm (30inch) high image has a mysterious and convoluted history; the first date of any certainty was its re-discovery in 1434, when lightning split open the chedi in which it had been enshrined.

When completed by King Rama V, the Golden Mount (Phu Kao Thong in Thai) dominated the otherwise flat city of Bangkok, although it must now compete for attention with modern skyscrapers. The golden chedi was built on an artificial hill, intended to reproduce a similar structure in the previous capital of Ayutthaya, but the notoriously soft earth of Bangkok delayed its completion for two generations of kings.

A view towards the Chaophaya River close to sunset takes in the spires of temples that dominate Rattanokosin Island, the royal nucleus of Bangkok (top). (Left) Flame trees at the height of the hot, dry season, flank Wat Ched Yod, one of Thailand's oldest temples, uniquely inspired by the Indian temple of Bodgaya. (Opposite) The wooden temple of Wat Chong Kham, in pure Shan style, once stood near the town of Ngao, but has been carefully moved to an open-air museum near Bangkok.

(Following page)
Wat Benjamabopit, the Marble Temple, was built by King Chulalongkorn in 1899, and is the most recent of the royal wats. Constructed from Carrara marble, and showing distinct European neo-classical influence, it was designed by Prince Naris, half-brother to the King.